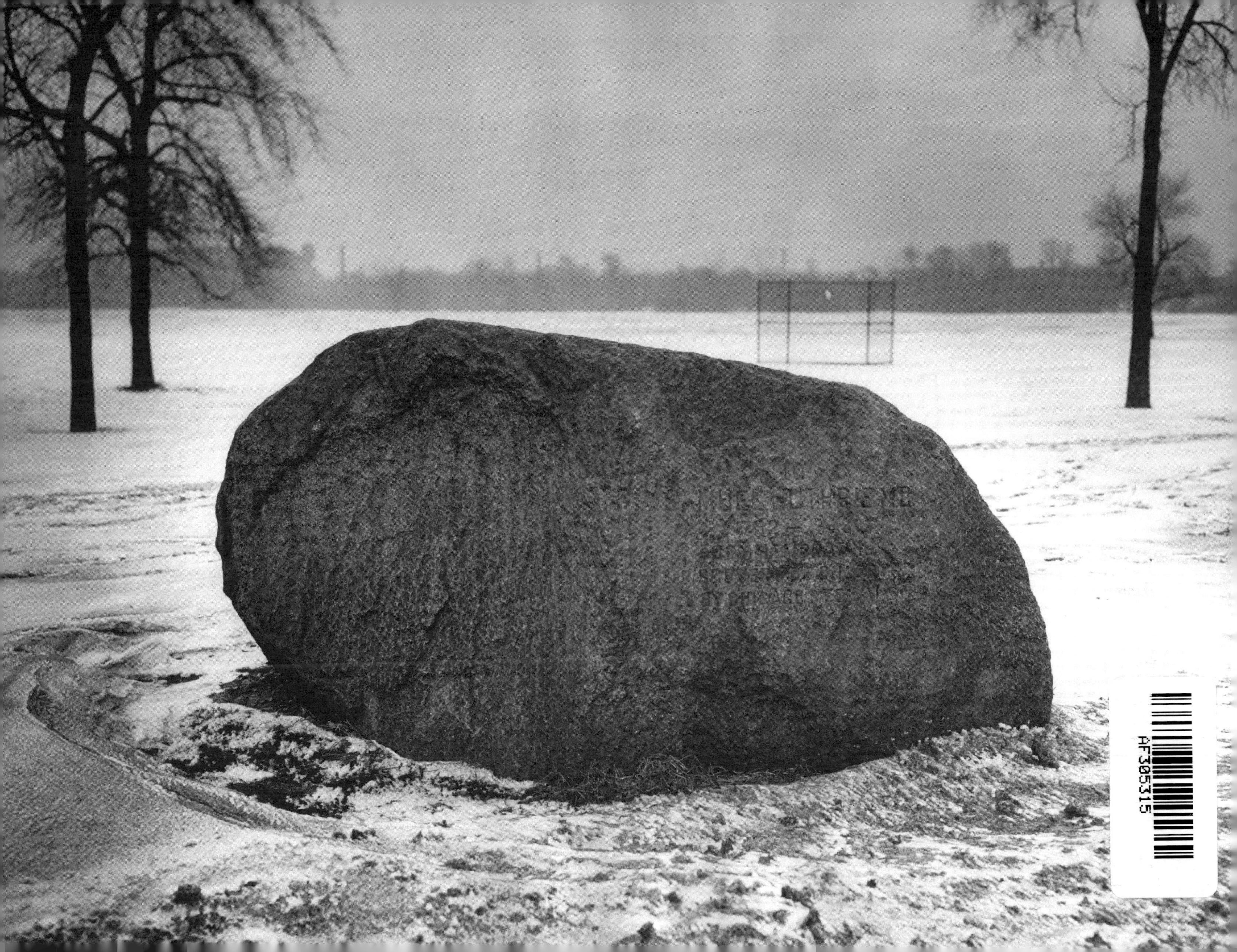

A
Rock zere
may Py
o Pre Tw...

This is Guthrie Rock in all its glory
. . . mired in the snow and mud north
of the Washington Park refectory at 56th
st. The glacier kicked it down here. We've
been kicking it around since.
FEB 5 1955

Dr. Samuel

PROJECT: Padding and decorative
...an make a headboard look like new.
...e hated my bed for five years, but on
...of furniture to replace, it was pretty
...d Lynne Frost, a homemaker who has
... part-time wallpapering and interior
...business.

...dboard. (

TE 5/11/83   EDIT

SLUG

RINTS TO   jeff

25 '83

OW-TO PROJECT

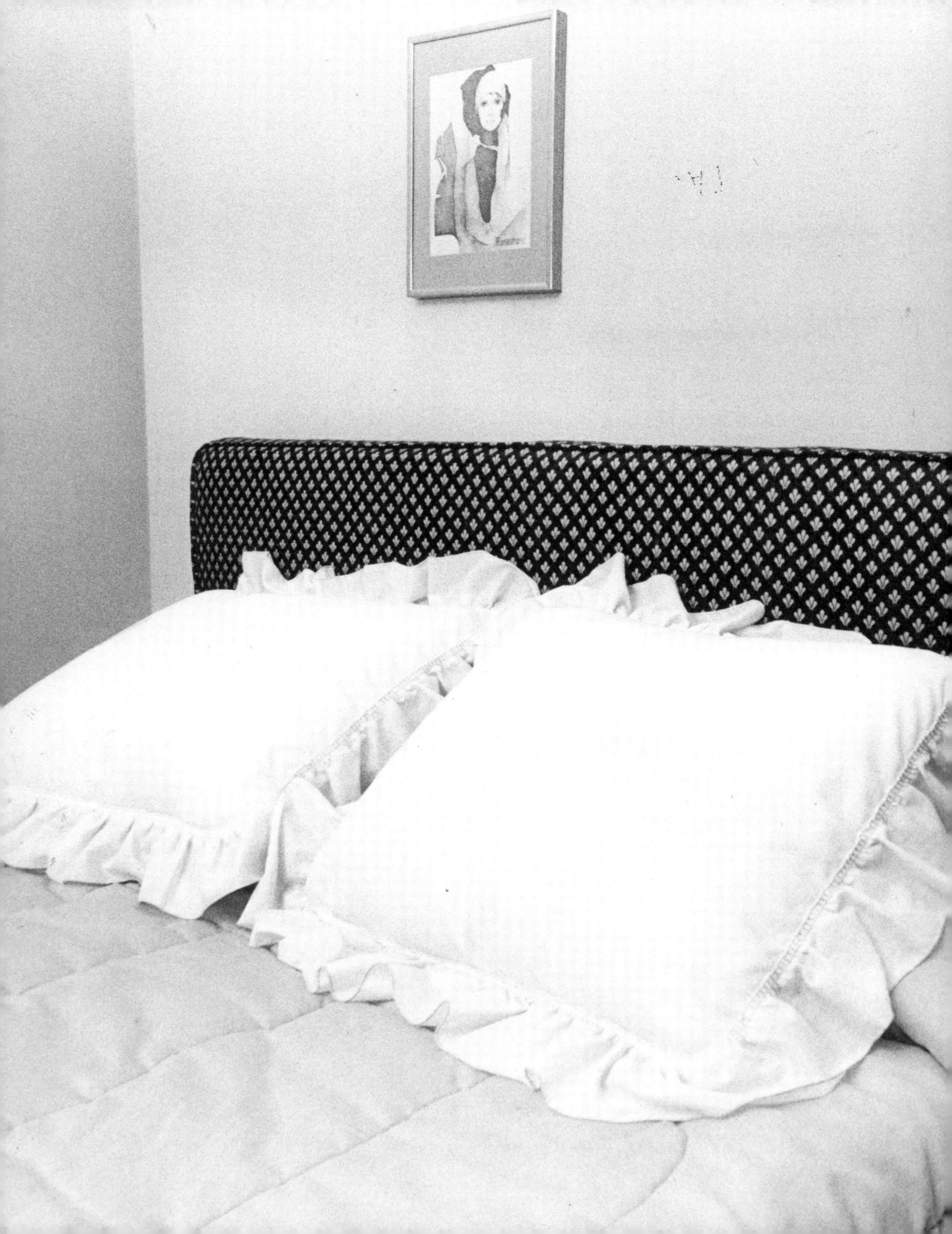

BROKEN VILLAS

These words are the beginning of a larger endeavour, written in response to a collection of physical photographs accrued over several years: single items purchased online, from auctions, from archival holdings. They are journalistic images, always black and white, whose narratives and informational tendrils have been snipped beyond legible connection with their original news accounts. The images are absurd, stoic, banal. They are chosen initially at whim, for the allure of their strangeness or their classic documentary capture. There are animals and fruit, ruined sites, models of human construction, figurative imprints, but never the physical body itself. Their grayscale development lends an effortless, exquisite beauty, slices of magic afloat. History is wilfully detached, with the intent of original portrayal mutated by interest. Their seduction is something akin to vibration, the disembodied experience of one fixed assemblage opened to the constitutive process of newly projected assemblages. After time spent in casual piles, these photographs have sifted themselves into a more focused selection of images that yield intimacy and noise. They are not ruin nor diagram, not elegy or theatre, but containers in the most explicit sense of having volume, devices that hold and withhold, and thus can be pried apart or newly conjoined. They are image-in-translation, forced evidence gifted to conceptual drift.

BROKEN VILLAS

Helen Marten

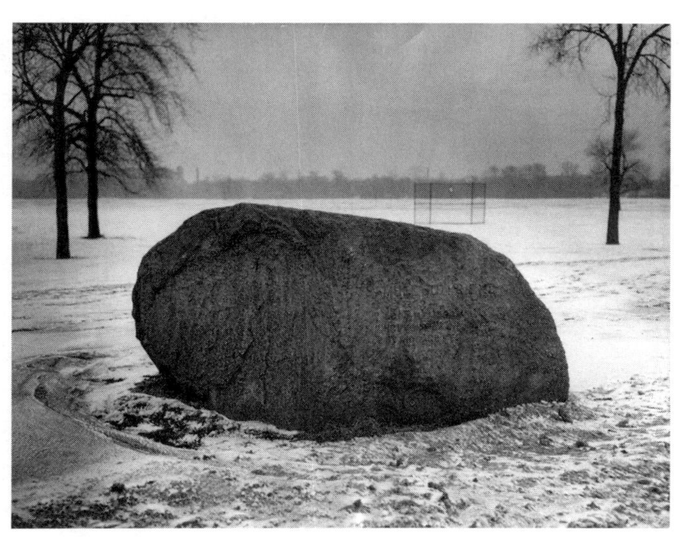

ERRATIC BOULDERS

The boulder of common imagination is too ungovernable to be coaxed by the human hand alone – too heavy, too hard, too large to make mobile. A lumpen side thickened with age, no welcoming ledge for the soft wreckage of a mortal's touch. The boulder is solemn, a powerful mineral hush; it is ancient dread and chemically sedimented history – a paradox of empirical and superstitious stratifications. Some boulders chance into the category of the *glacially erratic*, vast hunks of rock forced upwards by icy wind currents and deposited great distances from their familiar, taxonomical brethren, displaced and speechless; a species adrift. *Erratic boulders*: propelled without consent by the whirling arms of the Anemoi, minor male gods each assigned a cardinal direction, depicted as winged men or horses kept in the stables of seasonal storms: huffing sires of the immortal.[1] This glacial *erraticism* hints woefully at undisclosed mania inevitably akin to hysterical paroxysm – silent obedient matter jilted up out of the earth, hurled at whim, laid flat again, divested; tricked, disposed of: a dismally heterosexual performance.

More optimistically: a stone of wilful defiance, with a throbbing insatiability as wide and wild as the untamed glacier. Pleasure taken and pleasure abandoned. *Glacially erratic*. The boulder newly seeded, held deep and tight to the inevitability within, to the female power it wields. How then does the boulder mourn? It might be milked for the primitive grievances it contains, matter compacted and drawn up from one animal abyss to another. It is no coincidence that stones are deployed as table or tablet in the cemetery, as slabs to be laid as grave, externally visible text written, inaudibly parsed speech clasped within. The erratic boulder with its quiet performances of acquiescence, newly kneeling penitent. The boulder is not warm-blooded; it has no waist, no shoulders over which to drape an arm, and yet it hums with the soft sentience of blood. With all its obdurate heaviness it performs like a vault, wise and dense as a belly channelling the world's primeval vibrations. In this way, the boulder is never silent, but composed for the convenience of presentation. It performs the worn maternal act of the vessel's caress: it stores, it moans, it is silently equipped until labour is pressed upon it and it is there, assenting with its erraticism, its glacial clarity: stoic boulder, faithful shadow, manic rock.

Or, conversely, there is the boulder as hog, as wild toughened beast, linked etymologically to the Swedish dialectical *bullersten*, "noisy stone": an unruly, interrupting stone, dark sore thumb in the stream, this stone, cause of the roaring water around it. The boulder-disrupter, yet still no verbal sound it emits. Perhaps the stone is as mystical an avatar of unplottable realms of language or speech as the spectre. Its common romanticism, its unreasonable silence, its passionate absurdity – it contains everything and nothing at all. What might be assumed as unconscious material, is rather countless slivers of matter rubbed together with time and thermal energy to mark out thousands of notes of detail and biography. Just ask the stone, and it may not speak, but it will certainly signal. The twinkling rhapsodies of fish will testimony, the fish that swim around it when mountain snows melt and thundering streams escort more material adrift, these fish who drink amongst its currents, coax

[1] The winds gods of Greek mythology, the four main Anemoi are Boreas (North), Zephyrus (West), Notus (South) and Eurus (East).

it, smooth it. For a boulder is often softened, moulded, faintly sacred, faintly
wicked with its potential to wreck and destroy. Drop a boulder off a cliff and
a cartoonish disposal occurs, weight no longer true weight, but part of a new
staging of metamorphic objects that perform their gradations with gymnastic
flair. This dropped boulder is perfect fantasy, a possessed thing with the
magical elasticity of transposing mid-fall into so many other *things* it is not
– an anvil, a truck, a refrigerator, a bomb – facetious but lethal. The boulder
is now an object that swells and blows with symbolism, that thuds itself with
bovine will, is conjured all over with an unconscious alphabet, not a script,
but traced with fronds, with follicles, with phallus. Its exterior patterns can be
read like an astrology of innumerable lines, part precedent of hazard and fate,
part precedent of sinew, part precedent of image. Perhaps this transmutative
potential reflects a rock's classic alchemical value from crudest rubble to the
dignity of the divine.

    Human inclinations have indeed been kinder to the bodies of stones
than they have to the bodies of people. Roger Caillois named the pictorial
markings he found in stones, giving narrative expansion to the geometric,
skeuomorphic and illusionistic symbols that appeared on their faces: *The birth
of a child*; *Bird on a branch*; *Likeness of a face*; *Bony Monster*; *ghost*. A rotational
sequence of living and re-emergence – the boulder holding tight to all things
that touch it, from lightness through to dark, and all gradations of the rotational wheel in between. If the boulder were imagined as pot or cup or bowl,
it might be tapped to unfold other stories of harm and horror, of fortune or
gritted optimism. When moisture penetrates a rock, water seeps in freezing and
thawing penetrations. The boulder cracks and small veins open themselves to
intrepid flowers that root down and begin to bloom in its crevices. The formal
reversal of hard to soft is perhaps akin to Sisyphus's punishing stone with its
abstraction of defiance: from the logical gravitational tumble towards death,
derives the absurdly obstinate struggle to live. The boulder's volumetric density
is nectar after all, juice and sap, living fibres dormant but redeployed. A world
of signs and windows.

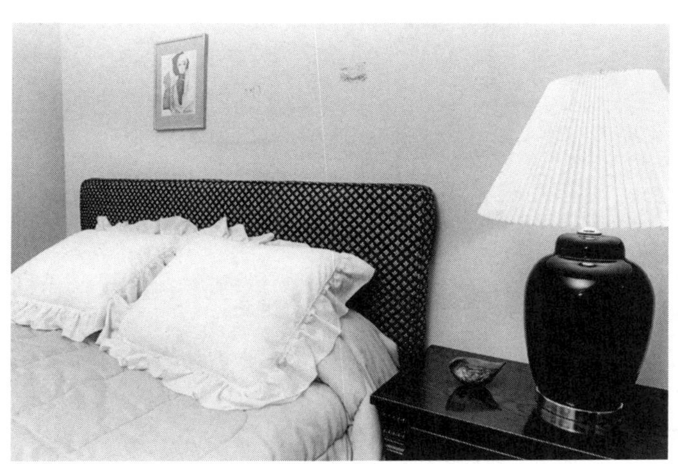

CRIMPED AROUND THE CROWN

The unkempt radius of a parking lot swells with decrepit things: single shoes and their gawping perished rubbers; a cat basket; a boxy soda machine empty and unquenching; a mattress thickened by its colonies of leaves and larvae. The underground car park is a portal of psychic or transdimensional fear, the Jungian or Escheresque landscape of relentless ups and downs, walls through the middle, shafts, stairs, shadows, and vacuum. These are the places in films where corpses are effortlessly made, where bodies are stuffed into trunks, chopped, shot through, or flattened under deliberate tires. Hot rubber and warm blood, paint and oil on chrome. The architectural perversity is symbolic of capital monumentality, of big low space generating the best expression of monetary value per cubic meter relative to the effort outsourced in creating what is marketed as "luxury commodity." The designations are elemental in their signaling, in their gridded possibility to expand in exponential rectangles. Cherubic children do not play here in fountains under sunlight, but rather the car park illustrates the abject man-made condition of relegating space to the "basement", devoid of real light. This is the state model and the family model crashing together under conditions that restore primacy to the fixed concepts of form, measurement, and mathematics: phobia and function issued into neat little squares with white line axiomatics that mark where to linger and for how long.

When the car park unfurls itself and issues invitation to drive in, this is the beginning of co-option into its architecture of symbolic persuasion. A nest at the side of the road, a pause, an event whose volumes simultaneously constitute assurance and nefarious exploit. The scenography echoes the creaking of a house at night, at once both familiar and a menacing prelude to intruder alarm. A vehicle or figure must mobilize itself into the lot – glide, walk, motor, run – so the generated fear is implicitly kinetic: it is one of jumping off, falling out, or being buried within. The horror of potential attack, or the simulation of a different kind of psychic abstraction (of simply losing your mind from its series of repetitive vanishing points that all look the same) looms large, in part because of the special spatial situation of ubiquity. This materiality is invested with multiple economies, such that meaning accumulates meaning; aggregates of so many lives lived. Patterns and diagrams emerge, but this is not purist architecture, rather the physiognomic characteristics of oppression-as-building.

In this simultaneous organization of words and surfaces, the danger is already specified and developed. Smell, or the image caricature of it – petrol spill, nosebleed tissue, desiccated dog shit – is all part of the theatre. The olfactory miracle of scent is that it unfurls itself with all the promised solidity of a physical wall, something to march into or claw against: the bitter fug of urine, hydrogen sulfide, the tease of just-passed perfume. Andy Warhol liked car parks and their Freudian capacity to paste seduction and despair into a single writhing lump. He pursued both automobile crashes and couture fragrance for the erotic volume of their violence. The car park, then, is apparatus, a model or a monster. It houses nomadic ambition and territorial influence.

It is no surprise that the typical contaminants of brownfield land include dry cleaners and gas stations, industries offloading spills of mixed corrosive toxicity: hydrocarbons, solvents, pesticides, lead, asbestos and other heavy metals. These materials level themselves at winter fogs and afloat in shawls of lethal mist people wrap up and continue. Tracts of housing and

industry so often lie side by side, patterned into portions of risk and divided
by the raggedy trails of chain link fencing. What is abandoned to roast in lethal
proximity, and what is privileged with the endeavor of clean breath is dis-
tinguished only by the slimmest probabilities. The body with all its semiotic
clawing is never far away: how many cubic feet of oxygen are contained within
the hollow diameters of scaffolding tube that hold fencing erect? How many
hands and lungs and nails have been busted rolling it out, dunking its slender
lengths into toxic pits of boiling zinc? This silvered spangled metal is galva-
nized in both skin and action: it is literally provided with a coating, but also
primed for "weather" in all linguistic possibilities – for the strange abstraction
of energy sources of both man and machine. The repetitive links of fencing
are expanded holes like the harlequin pattern of a conceptual erogenous zone:
a boundary desirous to cross precisely because it is closed off. Fingers waggle
through the mesh, yearn for the other side, and like skin there are pores of
a sort that remain open to receive trash or wind. How many sad weeds have
strangled themselves on this kind of fencing? Or the body forced up against
these links, thrown into them with a metallic rattle – this is the sound of figure
in both presence and negation.

The figures line up in houses as cars litter the streets, and in between
the shadings and layers of these expanses there are the inevitable bedrooms and
walls of domestic care. The pillowcase is a causal container, a motif of succor
whose proffer of classic laundered weaves suggests not burial but redemption.
Housing the body within an interpretation of pause, the pillow enlists itself
as yet another virtual site of chasing apparitions, rectangle upon rectangle in
staggering replication – another series of grids, a clean enclosing paddock, a
softness for the animal mind that drifts, that approaches through fog the door
of sleep. The mist is dense and white, as the pillow is dense and white, but
the animal head is still live, pulse empowered with demonstrative heat, and
through the white fog there is of course red, an avalanche of it, blood before
darkness. Blankness does not plunge out of it, but sound accompanied by all
its refrains: the hooting of a wraith or the voice of conscience with its layers of
depth and obedience. Crying and moaning are blended responses to pleasure
and pain. The body and pillow alike morph into something to be grasped at,
to press into, to hold captive. The pillowcase opens itself like a simple box to
all: to the rational souls, to the darkened compartmentalized souls.

The head is conditioned by its biology. It droops and surges, hardness
and fluidity determined by an ambient pressure that is essentially elastic. The
pillow is the miraculous conjoining device between a form moving through
horizontal and vertical motion, a bridge, softly propping. What cannot be seen
in literal terms are these small openings of madness laid out on empty cloth,
held internalized by the mind's ropes and springs, all the lines in transit that
express themselves not as text or image, but as shadows between the folds, as
invisible matter that hits the pillowcase and does not mark it, but ripples like
birds in the sky or fish in water. For the head, after all, is like the sky, a space so
untethered by one single geometry that there are no ontological edges left.

On the pillow, a prostrate body is a jumble of softly heated parts held
intact by a superficial layer of external skin, the epidermis, that provides barrier
and protection against invasion. The rhyme of membrane or sack is thus repli-
cated, *pillowcase* another poetic folding that offers itself to be possessed or filled.
The hair tangles down upon it, and it is soiled in the action – fatigue, rapture,
sickness, perspiration, hope – so much clinging of skin cell to fabric. On waking, the debris of sleep is brushed aside and the virtual images of dream, their
lucid seductions, the labyrinth, all of it converges just beneath the surface;
it lies *beyond* surface. In looking to find oneself after waking, there lingers the
subconscious fear of a visual agnosia that might be experienced when glancing

in the mirror and seeing a face neither neutral nor omnipotent, but simply
unrecognizable. This, too, is the perverse righteousness of violence. The picture
above the bed, the lampshade, the table ornament: each lies elemental and
stoic in supervision, sharing the roles of vigil and votive. They remind and
reassure with simple object-obstinance. Perhaps they even converse with
hushed severity, warding off the suspicions of ancient cosmology with its pre-
diction of stars raining down with curses. These items have been placed as
cues for simple reorientation: blue, the sky; green the grass; brown the bird.

The pillowcase offers itself to be claimed and re-scripted. It is stranded
between poles of reason, laid out internally – in homes, in hotels, in hospitals
– knocking and knocked upon, God and corpse with equal oddness, equal
magnetism, equal docile modesty. Prayers and proffers are flung into it; mouths
dribble and genitals swell then leak. In sleep, nothing tastes as it should:
skin like coal or cucumber; fruits like Vaseline; cement like marshmallow and
biscuit. The itinerary of feeling is specialised and new. Toys, knives, fruit, paper
– all things to crumple beneath the pillow and to become, via the sacrificial
focus of sleep, everything they are not. Atop the pillowcase, the focus is raptur-
ous: a vein in the temple spirals out and scrawls itself in additional figuration,
like finding a face in marble. The head on the pillow is a classic analogue of a
lone relic, a surrogate Baptist on a plate. But the dark romanticism of losing
one's head in simple passion or exhaustion is a wholly counter narrative to the
head lost in trauma, in war, in punishment, though extrajudicial persecution.
The eyeless tick or rampant mosquito who sucks until satiated, abundant
with blood, who drops to the earth only to die is nothing but a forsaken itch.
The pillow is a conduit to all these narratives; the gutter filled with coils of
emotional matter, with the folds of the soul. It is nothing like the street, and
yet ever so similar.

In Genesis 28, Jacob uses a rock for a pillow, dreaming the same night
of a ladder that extends from Earth to Heaven. With their fronded wings, his
angels pass their blessings from God to mortal. The design is symbolic: one
rung after another, rectangle following rectangle. The world is framed and
captured through each, every elevation surpassing ground, cliffs, clouds; a
stacking up of images like a pile of gathered pebbles. A pummeled stone brings
forth dust, ashes of the psyche given over to the wind. Pillow, then, from *pulvis*,
meaning dust, or from *pulvinus*, the soft mound or bulge at the junction of
a leaf with the axis of a stem. As ever, language returns with its poetic looping,
its condensed diagram: a bobbled head on an economical neck, bodily hubris
ever exerting itself upwards and towards the light. The Egyptians crafted their
own stone pillows for pragmatic and spiritual application, keeping heads pro-
tected, elevated from the floor to hold insects and bad spirits at bay. A starved
city rat might well tear a face clean off a head, hurtling down alleys with jaw-
bone or nose between its teeth. There is surely mystic doubling in this incident
of barbarity, the commotion of a mouth against a mouth, chewing, cradling,
screaming, relocating. The pillows of the Middle Ages suffered too from infes-
tation, abetting the atrophied and the poisoned, the spectacle of the headless
lost to misery and misfortune – and there again, the medieval epoch of horror
glints equally recognizable in contemporary terms.

Society is founded on fabric; its earthly interactions are hooked and
buttoned together. Cloth and how it structures defence or apparition belong
to the fictional battleground of the social body: a body that moves about across
the world's proscenium, rocked and bartered about, fucked, flung, delivered
out into the storm to face whatever molecules might stick. For fabric is politics,
it is property, emotion, rarely accident. Notch that fabric with the semantic
intent of a stich, and like the pleat or fold, it tugs at the importance of what is
or is not visible, of where the labour lies. The pleats on a domestic pillowcase

are a rhetorical comedy, baroque and belonging to the classical systematising
of value, to affirmation of class. The eighteenth century petticoat constructed
a similar defence, a small flag hung against injury and cleanliness – how much
it conceals and defends, and with what hilarity: a squeaked apology flapping
about the groin. Bedding's absurdly descriptive language loses itself in imagery:
envelope edged; crimped; scalloped; pleated; Oxford; square; housewife.
The dead and the living. All those pillowcases lined up in mind like an X-ray of
teeth, modules of undulation, row after row laid down, gnashing, opening up.
One single tossed pillow, and there is a skull stripped bare and washed to
brightness in the desert. Home to a head, once spongy and cavernous, left out
to waste like just another dry bone with its sockets of extremity, its shame that
comes in plurals with starling ease and multitudes of exhaustion.

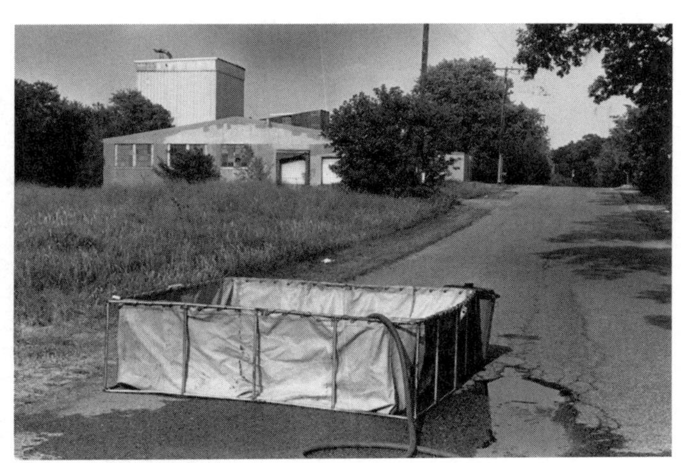

III

HOLE IN THE GROUND

Sunlight on an unpopulated scene lands on visible parts with a starkly lucid sense of portent. Light has a manic elocution, a competitive paranoia. It scatters itself and seeks a sound response, some language-in-the-seams activated by heat's rising kinetic surge. But over abandonment, sunshine holds paradoxical authority: unattended objects drift towards radical solitude, yet sit also underscored by the anticipation of potential fervour, of the allegorical unknown. The possibility for these shafting schemes of brightness is something akin to the waiting adder, the classic narrative deviator who slithers its own atomic delicacy over water, over rock, over earth, over vapour, coaxing, manoeuvring, and like a pointing dart, hinting at the suspicion that even in the natural world, there is no utterly clean transaction.

This scene is portioned into classic mythic archetypes: the unattended building and looming silo; the road that leads ever-away; the darkening trees with their canopies of lofty shade and silence. The nihilistic destination is towards danger, a descent away from rational explanation. Where light and heat should signal safe and soft, there is instead a lurking secret that illuminates the chemistry of matter's brutality. Composite material bristles, active in the sense of a tactile agency that desires to announce itself, that threatens outburst. Leak. Crack. Stain; Blood. Body. Container. What is non-pristine is haunted by atmospheric emanation. What is clean or tidy looks driven to insanity, singularly violent in the suppression of touch that charges the air around it. Recognisable markers dangle like threads to be pulled out, and from stillness there emerges the possibility for concentrated desire: the grandiose narcissism of the hidden spectator is to imagine, with pulsing greed, that the investment in these stories belongs to and is destined for them. Incidental exposure is the intrinsic psychological property of imagination.

The gleeful aim of extrapolation is submittance to this looming set of accentuated clues. Useless but poignant rubble abounds – a puddle, a flirtatiously hidden receptacle, the stealthy geometries of corrugated industry – each allowing compositions of a permeable set of images whose eclipsing riddles hold not clarity, but mystification. What access or lethal obfuscation do the roller shutters gesture towards? An apparatus of narcotic transformation? An archive of puzzles, of disappeared manuscripts, of words abandoned and unread? Incalculable litres of solidifying grey paint – the façade, after all, is toothed and tessellated with unfinished paintwork. And is this open blindness of narrative ambiguity not part of the very paradox of the hole? An excavated seam in the earth is a simple invitation to conspiracy: undone cavity; magical escape; sucking pleasure; inexorable vacuum; wretched jail; exhausted refuge.

Excavation necessarily requires the removal of earth from one point to another. Scooping at the ground or breaking into cement is an act of exertional mathematics – positive accumulation engineered through negative subtraction. Perhaps the eye's own pupillary light response – its contraction and dilation – is an analogy for the ironic sabotage of this perceptual mode, the eye projecting itself beneath ground, seeing more in darkness as the eyeball's proffered bowl expands to accommodate the dirt that fills it. Matter is examined via analysis' classic attraction and repulsion valences, and the deep hole of the eye's iris becomes itself a threshold of withheld infinities, another potential containing device, another well to dip into, and a biological model geometrically

linked to openings and borders. The contrary mechanics are another reverse
equation: wideness perversely likened with night or dark, and smallness
with illumination.

Archaeology aims to perform its own spatial hollowing with painstaking
sensitivity. Sometimes bones are unearthed, sometimes the enhanced durables
of industrious civilisation: a jug's lip; a button; cutting flints; a wooden comb.
Sometimes jewellery or cloth. Foundations are rediscovered, diagrammed back
into focus to provide structures for passion, for commerce or death. The ethical
vow of preservation is solemn but entangled with a performance of acquisitive
hoarding, a strange kind of social ablution, portions of peoples humped
without ceremony into crates or cardboard: the ambition is figurative, but the
interpretation may be crude or abstract. If the discovery is harsh or criminal,
the narrative still spools with inevitable delay, data measured foremost for
its empiricism, its exact place in the extensive trespass of unearthing the past
to know the future. Even a smashed skull is open to interpretive questioning,
subject again to the delirious tactile clock of things buried beneath ground.
The discoverable nodes of voice and consequence are part of a sedimentation
that does not always necessarily sit on the surface. Perhaps the mossy sod
of a peat bog or the shale of Jurassic sandstone is as surface akin to horizontal
lines on a musical score – images of singular flatness that bristle with livid
evidence of potential noise; the rat tail flicking over ground with rhythm and
reverberation.

A hole in the countryside might be considered incidental, a warren or
burrow to blind beasts. Like archipelagos budding up and out of the sea, these
holes belong to the circulatory tunnelling of nature's active crust, lived-in
islands and caves, or more speculatively as pits for the cosmos's psychic ashes.
A hole ringed with tarpaulin signals intervention, interference via plastics or
hoses, and a volume therefore subject to the infinite drift of synthetic science,
of folklore or linguistic tale. The fence around the hole lures the imagination,
the beginning of a message broken by this barrier made between expression
and delivery. The tarpaulin is undoubtedly flecked, signalling with involuntary
reticence: shadow stains, with blood, with oil? Ever the vital compounding
fluids of war and power. The total body of economy is stealthily at work here,
fixing, redrafting, repairing. The hole is social aggregate, the granular gravity
of the core, a tactic to conceal the falling apart. Perhaps most humbly this hole
holds breadcrumbs and orange peel. Perhaps white pebbles with all their fretful
signalling, for it only takes one hungry witch to construct a lure and delude
with crumbs.

A mad stone is a stone that draws out poison, heals wounds, detoxifying
inch by inch. A mad stone must never be bought or sold; the mercenary tactics
negate the strength of its healing powers. These stones are found lodged deep
in the intestinal folds of cud-chewing animals, passed out of bladders and
buried in sand or soil. Soaked with milk and pressed against living veins to heal
rabid bites and Poison Ivy, a mad stone is another kind of hole: an orifice that
has swallowed like a sin-eating mouth, curdled around poison, gagging on its
own conscious will to live, and in that ingesting, the hole of its own conceptual
gullet is turned inside out and seals itself – a hole to a stone and back again;
cough and spit and swallow.

A contemporary hole, especially one dedicatedly obfuscated by fence
or border or barrier, is a blemished site. Common metropolis aesthetics prefer-
ence an orderly surface without the interruption of cavities one may fall into,
without craters that disrupt infrastructural expediency, harassing the succinct
route, collecting trash or vermin. The hole in the earth is part of the game of
distraction. It is a sore, a medieval blight on the axes of contemporary progress.
And like a pox, any dent in the skin of a roughly unified flatness will collect

liquid: a hole in the ground opens itself naked to city flagellation, to flood, to the fluid metrics of drip and discharge, and thus the implicated modes of drainage, floatation and filtration. A hole into which one cannot see is a space that behaves like a consciousness tasked with rooting out an eclipsed riddle. This is subterranean geology that is neither moral nor scientific, but uneasy. In this way, there are secret plots that ask who or what has done this digging: machine, animal, human, ghost?

Perhaps a hole in the ground cannot escape an inevitable capitalist tug – rubble-architecture formed to fill up again, excavated so as to network, to plumb, to mine, to bury. Holes belong to grand emergency, attached to the pathology of the victim, to a city's matrix dissolve and secretly dug where the earth's pores ought to suffice, where things have learnt to walk that ought to crawl.[2] Passive curiosity swiftly conjures the horror of a corpse, not a softly naked pup splashing in a tub, but a soaking skin, a dead worker's body itched off in madness and sloughed towards something othered, something beyond the localised obsession with the planet. What other traumatic geologies, then, beside a suicide or a homicide might nestle below: a pit of mice or rats with their vectors of epidemic; dust newly dispersed and wholly contagious; a perpetual motion machine defying all thermodynamic laws, decay building without creation; an unnameable darkness of broken stars.

Look hard enough into a chasmic hole and finally there is the sea, magnetism mapping sweet groundwater that flows newly salty and ferric as the distance down increases. A deep hole in the ocean, a dark staring hole, is a metaphoric iris, another eye as seeing-blackness that gapes up at the moon, and performs the greedy swallowing of its ludic vanilla light, blinking once with intuition, then again with enlightenment. The rhythm of that huge blue ocean: it lies wide and splayed out, turned upwards, full of wise wind and current; its physics are sacred.

Rolling heavy within the deepest ocean holes, there lurks the octopus drenched and drunk with spray, one rubbery tentacle entwined with agitation against the ocean's floor, squeezing, exhuming, moving in weighty procession with other lesser sea folk, the lobsters, the clams, the oyster, the abalone. The gigantic octopus is libidinal and rebellious, parentheses and bubble all at once. In Hokusai's *The Dream of the Fisherman's Wife*, the octopus strangles and seduces with enveloping moisture, mouth over genitals, tentacles in and around all holes. The mandible is soft and greedy, suckers assimilated with flesh and skin, supporting spine and head, the draftsman's inked line deftly threaded and masterful. The dark eyes of the octopus are halved like two perfectly black semicircles. The eyeball is sliced and clean: united together, both halves of this blackness form one final hole – a borehole trepanned directly into the mind of myth, towards new lust, to suck and suck and suck some more, as oil, after all, and pleasure, is the ooze which makes the world scream.

2 H.P. Lovecraft, *The Festival*

Broken Villas by Helen Marten
Published by Bricks from the Kiln (BFTK~BV), May 2024
Printed in an edition of 500 copies
Edited by Helen Marten, Harriet Moore & Matthew Stuart
Designed by Matthew Stuart
Printed by Tallinna Raamatutrukikoda
Copyright © author
ISBN 978-0-9956835-9-4

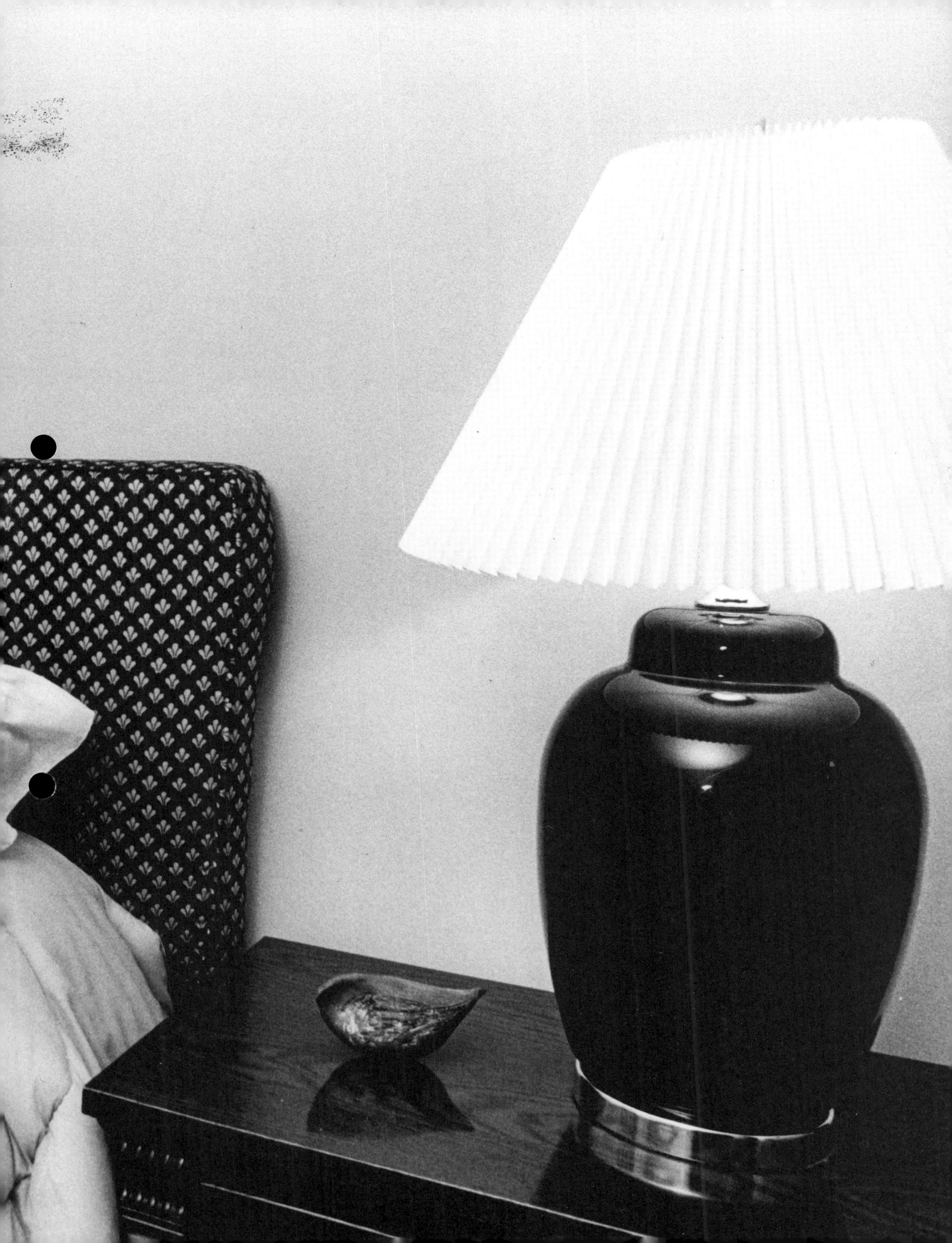

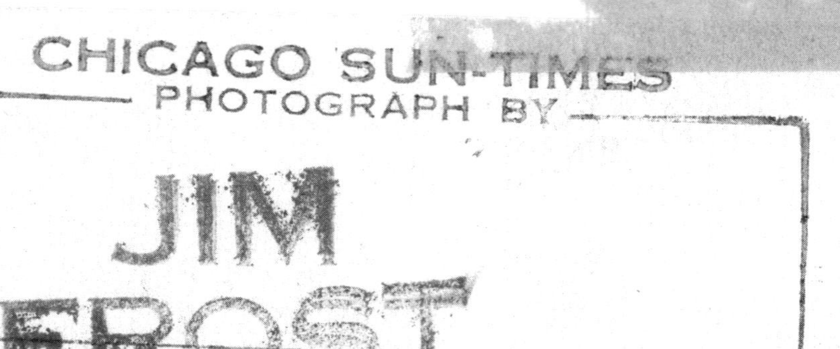

Beds

THE
fabric
"I ha
my list
low," s
her ow
paintin

Under new patterned fabric is a 16-year-old Mediterranean style he

APHER	Jim Frost	
N	elk grove	
R	J. Moore	

SAT J

upholstered bed headboard for

Photographer Jim Frost, 1988

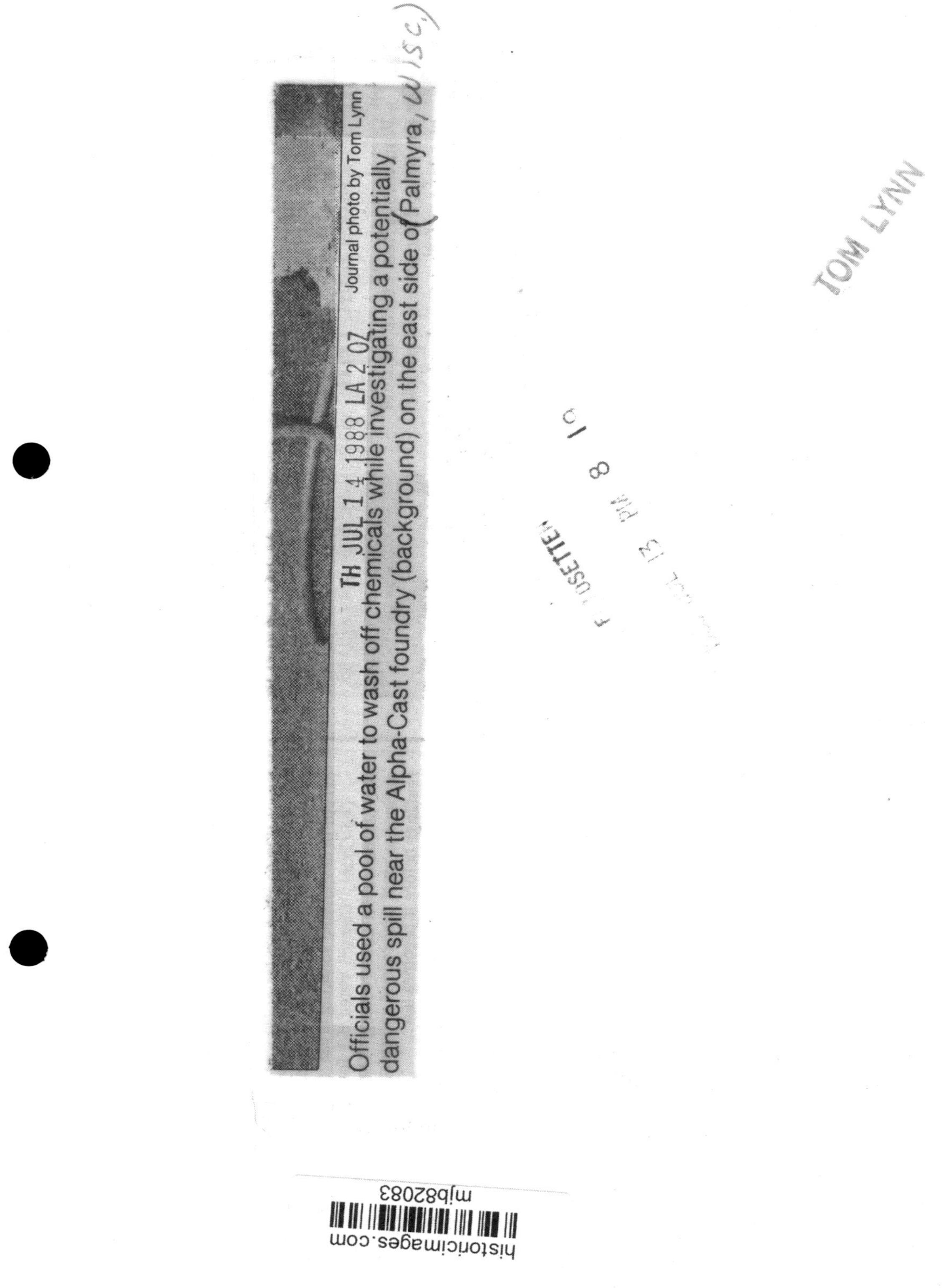

TH JUL 1 4 1988 LA 2 07   Journal photo by Tom Lynn

Officials used a pool of water to wash off chemicals while investigating a potentially dangerous spill near the Alpha-Cast foundry (background) on the east side of Palmyra, Wisc.

Photographer Tom Lynn, 1988

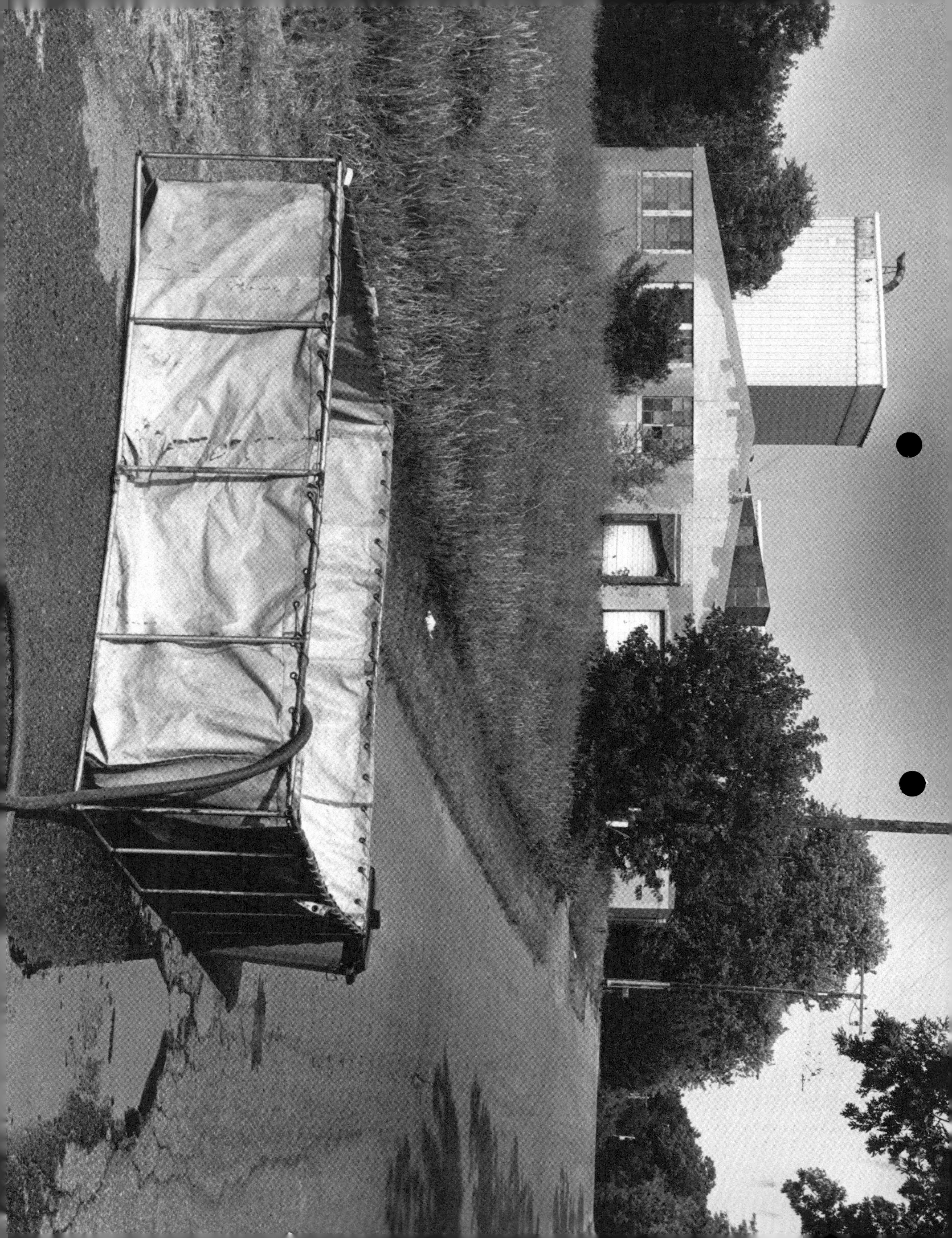